You're okay

My Poetic Journey Through Life's Struggles, Realizations, and Healing

Scott Thornton

Book production by MysticqueRose Publishing Services LLC

ISBNs:

979-8-9986803-0-4 - Paperback

979-8-9986803-1-1 - Hardcover

979-8-9986803-2-8 - Ebook

979-8-9986803-3-5 - Audiobook

Contents

Part I: Hopelessness — The Long Dark Night 6

An Intermission in GRIEF — Chronicles of Grandma 26

Back to Hopeless 38

Part II: Spark — A Dawning Arises 71

Part III: The Journey — Dancing Between the Dark and the Light 132

Part IV: Hopeful — A Genesis of Understanding and Peace 163

About the Author 230

Acknowledgements 232

Art Index 234

Resources for Healing 238

Dear You,

I have not walked in your shoes, and I'm not familiar with your exact situation, but I can bet that during your journey, you've probably felt lonely, felt heartbreak, and experienced pain.

I've had a similar journey. I've felt alone before. I thought I was lost. I've experienced emotional pain and heartbreak. I've felt unworthy. Unredeemable. I was sure I was the only one feeling these things. I've made many missteps and misjudgments. I didn't know where to turn. I didn't know what to do. Hated how my life was and who I was being. How I was behaving.

Finally, I couldn't take it. I didn't want to be this version of myself anymore. I didn't want to feel like this every day. And so, I looked. I searched for something that spoke to me. Something, someone, that talked to my soul, for something that made me feel a glimmer of hope. I simply started by Googling how I was feeling.

"What to do if you feel lost or helpless?"

"Who can help with changing your life?"

I poured through the results, searched more, and finally found people whose messages resonated with me. Coaches and therapists. Then, I realized I had to do something that I wasn't sure I could do. I had to be brave. I had to open up. I had to ask for help, and I did. It was probably the best decision of my life. I found out I wasn't alone. I wasn't the only person feeling this way, having feelings of depression and isolation.

My coaches and therapist said it happens to many people, really to everyone, at some point. It's normal. It's life, and when you fight that, don't allow the feelings in, to bury them, well that just buries you deeper and deeper.

So, I may not know your circumstances or what exactly is causing your disease, but I'm guessing you can relate. Our roads might not be the same, but they can be parallel.

I want you to know you are not alone. Others, myself included, have felt similar. Been in similar places. Situations. If you want it to change all the feelings, the despair, there has to be a change. It's a choice. Your choice. It requires that change. Change isn't good or bad; it's only change.

You would never see the sun nor moon if the day never changed. Never see spring flowers or winter snow if the season doesn't change. Change is what you make it. It's necessary to evolve, to have a new mindset, and to understand your feelings. To get out of the space that is making you so unhappy. There are people out there who want to help and facilitate the journey. You just need to look and have courage.

Consider this a testimony of mine, that there is hope. Change is possible. With courage, resilience, and hard work. Hard work on yourself, on your mindset, and on your perception. Consider this a love letter to you.

You are thought of, cared about, and supported.

You're okay.

We all have work to do. The sooner you start, the sooner you can start to see life differently. The sooner things can feel different. What I really hope you get out of this book of poems is you are not alone. Things, life, can be different with hard work on yourself, your perception of self and others, and the ability to handle change.

It is my wish that these poems help you feel connected and hopeful, and help you realize that there is help should you put the work in.

Love,

~Scott

It's only lonely

If your eyes look

In one direction

And your hand

Your heart

is closed

Part 1: Hopelessness

The Long Dark Night

Ooze

All these thoughts and feelings

They ooze and seep

Through the cracks

Of my being

I share them with the world

Because I don't know

If I'm the only one

That is feeling this way

Is it normal

Or should I even care

I just want

To fit in somewhere

Jumbled and mixed up

My mental state is in flux

A moment's peace is elusive

I'm not sure how this ends up

See

My face says there's a gentle song
Playing behind my eyes
But truth be told
I'm screaming
At the top of my lungs
Scratching and clawing
At my frontal lobe
A riot playing inside my mind
A cacophony
The surface may seem serene
But underneath
There's chaos and trouble
My volume is turned up to 99
I'm begging and pleading
On the inside
For you to see through
My glassy eyes
Barely holding back the tears
Silently
Dry weeping
And this smile that hides
A litany of profanity
Curses I want to blurt out
Instead
I just nod my head
In compliance with you
And society
When all I really want
Need
Is for you to see into me
Selfless intimacy
Let me feel safe to be the real me
Intimately
And for you to say
I'm here
It'll all be okay
Even if I know it won't
I want to be able to bleed through
My papier-mâché exterior
Tear the strips away
With my inhibitions
Let me be revealed at last
All I want is to be seen
No more pretending
Only Authentically
Can I find the strength
To be the version
Of me
I've always wanted to be
Let you in
So you can see
The genuine me

Messy

When you look at me
Can you hear me screaming
Inside of my head
At the top my thoughts
Can you feel the tears
Streaming out
Falling like a waterfall
On the inside
Never running dry
When you look at me
Can you see my cracks
Fractured parts
Broken me
I have no golden glue
Can you see past this whole
Understand all my pieces
I need someone who can
Because I can't
I no longer see the beauty in me
Disillusioned
Mind and soul
Where do I start
Fixing this messy me

Why

Why don't I know
My own feelings
They are there
Existing
But I am not present for them
They alarm me
Alien
It is as if feelings
are a different language
Foreign
And I cannot translate them
They are electric
Shocking me
They are heavy
Pulling me down
They are fluid
Filling me
Drowning me
I wake from feeling
Gasping
Confused
I need a guidebook
A map
To help me
Navigate
This wilderness
Of emotions
That leave me lost
In myself

Wiped Away

I'm no longer here

I've faded away

Nothing left

A water stain

Or a ghost

This is what happens

When unattended

By self

For self

I thought

You would save me

Could save me

Instead

Neglected, I vanish

From perspective lost

Formless in opinion

In my reality

Wiped away

Like a forgotten memory

Because I wanted someone

To save me

When I could have saved myself

All along

Lonely

I am so lonely
Standing in this room
Surrounded by these people
Standing next to me
The distance in my mind
Between us
Might as well be
A million miles

I am so lonely
Separated emotionally
There is no connection
Even if we touched
Nothing passes between us
I can see their lips
Moving
But the words make no sense
It's all lost in translation
Emptying my heart

I am so lonely
Desolation is all I see
The world barren
Torching my soul
Until I'm burnt
To the end of this rope
I let go

There's nothing left
Between us

I'm all alone

Boxed up

Those thoughts and feelings
That you boxed up
In your head
To keep hidden
That you were ashamed of
Hoping you'd never
Come across again
They're back
Reaching out
Of that box
Pulling you in
Fighting fear with fear
Just creates more fear
Same for shame, regret, and anger
Open your box
Let the hidden out
Work through it
Deny it
And you'll never be free
Accept and integrate
The weight lifts
Nothing to hide
Freedom ensues
Use your boxes for presents
Not shame

Respite

I'm feeling
Everything
I'm drowning
In an ocean
Of feelings
I can't keep treading
These emotions
Dragging me under
Hard
To breathe
When choking on all of these
Sentiments
Foreign
And strange
Fearful to let them all in
Smothering in the panic
Of how to navigate
My way through
I just need a respite
From my weary mind
Something
Somewhere
I can rest
Peace
Bring me home
Alone
That behavior
Brought back painful memories
Reminding me
That despite being surrounded by
people, even loved ones
I'm all alone
Not to be hopeless or negative
I'm not a pessimist
But it seems
My tender heart is ground ashes
I'm a sensitive soul
Thoughtless actions and words
Cut me to the quick
Reminding me
That I am all alone
Back to my isolation
Heart not for sale
My emotions
Overwhelmed
Putting myself out there
Doesn't work
It leads to hurt
Frustration
And more tears
Than I condone
I'm better off
Alone

Ego

I am the rise of anxieties

And the fall of inhibitions

I am the conqueror of civilizations

And the destroyer of self

I am the lies stealing your strength

And the adrenaline saving your life

I love you

But I won't let you grow

I want you to stay with me

As you always are

Never changing

Never risking

The best-laid intentions

That destroy your future

I am always there whispering in your mind

Tripping you

Making you small

Listen to me

And you'll never fall

Because I keep you from climbing

To the heights you can go

I am your ego

Devoid

I do not know how

To navigate this life

This mind

How do I survive

How do I breathe

I feel nothing

I am devoid of emotion

Caring

It seems that everything has lost its meaning

Everywhere I look

It is as if I am in a snowstorm

Dirty

Trod over

No pristine white left

Only the gray fills my sight

Like I am surrounded by another dimension

An alien in this world

How can I bring color back to my world

How do I come alive again

When I am nothing but a void

Inside me

An Intermission in GRIEF

Chronicles of Grandma

My grandma was the most meaningful, special person to ever touch my life. She taught me unconditional love, acceptance, and the power of smiling and laughing. She was wonderful, loving, delightful, funny, and just plain old goofy.

There are no words that can describe what she meant to me and still does to this day. Yet, I forgot this for a time in my life. A far too long period. Her death devastated me. I did not have the emotional bandwidth nor the tools to understand or deal with her passing.

So, I ignored it. Didn't think about her. When I did, or had to, I couldn't talk. Tears would instantly well up. I fought those tears off and moved on, putting her and all the beautiful times I had with her, and the lessons in life and loving with an open heart aside.

I did not grieve. I did not feel the loss. I did not cope. It changed me as a person doing this. Not for the better.

It took me over twenty years to seek help, work through all the pent-up sorrow that had turned to rage and anger, and just feel all the pain and loss.

To accept. To move through all of the emotions around her passing and what that loss meant to me. To be able to open my heart fully and love without restriction again. It allowed me to remember her, her love, and everything she left behind with me.

I can now share her and her beauty with the world, my friends, and most of all, with my children.

If there is one lesson I learned from this; do not wait. Do not push your feelings and pain down. Feel. Grieve. Acknowledge all of it, and then move through it. It is not easy, but it is healthy and needed. Live again. Don't be a prisoner of it.

Do I wish I had done this sooner? Sure, but I do not want to live with regrets. I didn't, that is just a fact. Nothing will change it. I would rather be grateful. Grateful that I found a way out of that darkness. Grateful that I can now remember her lovingly and share her stories. Grateful she was such a huge part of my life and such an influence on what makes me me. What is grief but loss unacknowledged, feelings suppressed, and love unrealized.

I know now that you will live on forever in me, my children, and their children, living by the loving examples you set. As I sit here writing this, tears in my eyes not held back, know this: I love you, Goofy Grandma.

Grief PT 1

I don't know

How much further

I could fall

Into the depths of my despair

The world lost all its color

To me

There were no more smiles

No more dances

Nothing … nothing mattered

My heart was gone

The world, my world, had changed

I was hollow, alone

I still desperately ache

For one more talk

One more meal

Your unconditional love

Everything

Will never be the same

To this day

I still can't even say your name

Grief PT 2

You would think

I became a better man

You would have thought

I'd live each day

To your standard

To make you proud

I did not

I failed, I stumbled, I sank

I let my grief, my pain

So much pain

Be my banner

Fill my heart

You never even met my children!

Unfair! Cruel! No one cared

No one even saw

My only trust

My one believer

My lasting faith

Was gone, returned to dirt

Filling me with dust

Only remnants left of who I was

My essence shattered, broken

Forevermore

Grief PT 3

The wound is still there
Laid bare
Open, hurting
God is unfair
I am still mad at Him
Angry! Why did He let you suffer!
The queen of His faith
Sayer of prayers
The best woman I ever knew
Her cross so heavy to bear
Yet, like the Angel she was
The burden was not too much
You shined, you loved, you rose
While I anguished without you
Not thinking of you, forgetting for years
It hurt too much
The pain too strong
I, too weak
For far too long
But there is hope
I am not healed
But I have started

I think of you more
I miss you so
I let myself grieve, occasionally
I let myself cry, over you
Tears flowing, then, after a while
I smile
About you, for you, loving you

Guide

Through you
Your Holy Spirit
Your grace flows into me
It's been here for years
Since you ceased
Your time on this plane
I didn't see it
Feel it
Until now
It took time
But now
I am feeling your power
Through the words I say
The actions I take
Thoughts I have
I am grateful
For your patience
For leaving this present behind
For me to find
Eventually
The love you gave
And Continue
To send
It permeates

My life

My vision

Everywhere I look

Everything I feel

The lessons of kindness

Joy

Thank you, Grandma

For the unconditional

Love you showed

Taught

You'll Always be

My guiding light

I only need to remember

Where to look

Lighthouse

My love
For you
Has made me a prisoner
Of my pain
Since you left
I've drowned in anguish
And grief
When I even acknowledge
Your absence
Most days
I pretend that
You never existed
I know
You would never wish
For me to feel this way
You would want me to continue
To love and laugh
Live a life of wonder
And joy
But you were so important
So vital
Like air
To my survival
I am lost
Adrift
Deadening myself
Without you
You were my lighthouse
In the storm of life
A beacon of love
Safety
Acceptance
With your light gone
I am lost in an ocean
Of myself
Self-doubt and loneliness
Circles me
Like sharks
Blood in the water
Waiting on the kill
No shore in sight
No safe port
Only wave upon wave of grief
Leaving me day after day
Gasping for breath
But exhaustion overwhelms
Tiring
How much longer
Can I tread this feeling
Before slipping under
Those sorrowful waves

Ache

There is an ache
That sits in my chest
But resonates down to my soul
Echoing through my body
My consciousness
My life
Lifetimes
Always searching
For someone
Something
To ease it
To fill it
Knowing it's really me
Myself
That can ease this suffering
The sadness
The pain
This ache
I have all the pieces
I can see the puzzle
But still
Unable to fit it
All together
So frustrating
Disappointing
Tearful even
When you have lived with it
For so long
It becomes normal
Routine
But it's not
Shouldn't be
Expected
Occasionally, the answer is there
Within sight
Just out of reach
So close
And then
Disappears
Making the ache
So much deeper
With each heartbeat
Reverberating the ache
Into the hollowness
Of my being
This aching
Dreaming
One day of its release
From the prison of my mind
Into the universe
Free
To drift
Like stardust
Into my awareness
Healing
At rest
Whole

Weightless

I don't know

What to do with this

This grief

This sorrow

This pain

It weighs me down

It's like lead

Poisoning me

Seeping

Into my bloodstream

Contaminating

My mind

My spirit

Slowly killing me

From the inside

I love you

I want to remember you

But I don't want

To die with you

How do I release you

How do I set you free

How do I live

Weightless

Free

Back to Hopeless

Buried Alive

I'm stuck

Can't get out

Things are so heavy

I can't move

Weighing me down

Can't breathe

Unmanageable

Feel like the world is ending

I'm buried alive

In my own head

Under my own thoughts

Else

I no longer know how to be happy

Was I ever?

I doubt it

It's all been a facade

Imaginary thoughts and feelings

To get me through the day

The Year

My life

I want to

Be happy

I don't know how

My thoughts betray me

Fight me

Was I conditioned?

Not loved enough?

It seems so simple for so many

Not me

A constant struggle

How does it end?

Can I make it stop?

I don't even want to be happy anymore

I just want this to stop

This pain

This misery

The sadness

This feeling of just not being enough

To go away

Should I become Alice?

Disappear down a rabbit hole?

Take colored pills

To be something else

Somewhere else

Someone else

If this is a test

I'd fail

I don't have the answers

Let me cheat off someone

Copy their answers

But one size does not fit all

And their test is different than mine

I don't know how to be happy

I don't even know how to be me

Straining

I strain for air

Each breath is a gasp

My lungs are on fire

As my mind begins to panic

The weight of expectations

Sits like an elephant

On my chest

As my world narrows

And darkness crowds the corners

Of my vision

Somewhere in the shadows of my mind

I begin to wonder

Can I endure

The pain that comes with each racing heartbeat

Is this the end

Then I realize

It is just the beginning of another day

In this life

That is mine

Blame

I blame you

Or him

Or her

I blame anything or anyone else

Point the finger anywhere

But here

If I acknowledge

I have to take responsibility

Do the work
Change
But I'm scared in place

What The Heart Feels

Strongly

Passionately

When it breaks

Into a thousand pieces

With all its cracks

And scars

Will it ever

Be able

To feel the same

Again

Over and Over

Sitting here
With a drink in my hand
This song
Got me on the feels
Where'd I go wrong
Feeling alone
Almost done
Pour another
This beat
Got me feeling
Why can't I have her
So I get no one
Grab the bottle
Finish it off
This guitar
Has me crying
Tears asking
Why can't I have
What they do
Sitting here
One last drink
Before I pass out
Sleep, rinse, repeat
This song
Got me wondering
What's wrong with my life
Just playing
The same old track
Over and over

Glue

I think I'm broken
In ways that can't be fixed
In my mind
Down in my heart
Something diseased
Something sick
I don't feel good
Something is twisted
Love has left blood
Across my eyes
Stained my vision
Painted it skeptical
I no longer believe
In true love
One love

Fractured displays of affection
Caring
Warped my senses
And self
Something's not right
In my head
In my belief
There are cracks
All over in here
In me
Someone hand me some glue
I have a lot of work to do
Putting it all back together again

Sadness

I'm drawn to sadness

But not by choice

I think I was born into it

It comforts me

like a cozy blanket

Or a warm jacket

Expressing it comes easy

Inspires my imagination

Sadness is the steam

That drives my engine

Happy is good

Though awkward

Ill-fitting

Like a suit

A size too small

It covers you

But just doesn't look right

Melancholy has been

A second skin

Comfortable

Like a fire in the hearth

Or a fondly remembered photo

It just feels like home

Bulb

I let the light in my mind

Burn out

Burnt down to the filament

Charred

Broken in half

My eyes

Dull and glossed over

Barely a spark

Can I recharge

Do I want to

What will it take

For this flicker

To become a full shine

Sometimes a broken spirit

Like a light bulb

Requires a change

Look

Don't look too close

You might see through

The illusion I project

That I'm okay

Everything is fine

And I am well

Truth is

I'm a big mess

I do my best

But I'm slipping through the cracks

Facade

The facade
The smile
Parts of it are real
Me
Bits and pieces
Here and there
Enough for people to
Think they know
Know me
My life
But no
Not the real me
That's been the choice
My choice
But the poetry
That's me
Real
Raw
Unfiltered
The bleeding
The open
Unhealed
Gaping wounds
That have formed my world
My distrust
My perverse yearnings
The screaming agonies
Of every word
Action
Lie
I've endured
Survived
And lived to tell
These words
These feelings
Those moments
Are the truth
Are me
Told through the distortion
Of being

Crooked

How shall I traverse

This crooked land

Fraught with perils

And demons

Shadows that grab hold of you

And refuse to let go

How do I cross

Such a confusing convoluted landscape

With hidden dangers

Behind pretty pictures

And picturesque scenery

That lulls you into a deluded sense of safety

But Pitfalls around every situation

Melting mindscapes

And false gods

How do I escape this place

I walk in every moment

Of everyday

How do I escape

My own mind

Alive

Or even sane

Dissolve

Like sugar

In coffee

Or some other drink

But not sweet

I dissolve

In life

Disappear

Soured on the foul words

Actions

Of this world

Is there kindness left?

Hope still alive?

Or has it dissolved

In the madness of today?

Can't

I just can't do it

Energy so low

Exhaustion rushes in

Overwhelmed

Despair

Attitude shitty

Outlook bleak

This is going to be a deep hole

To climb out of

Unhappy

I feel no happiness

No joy

I am beget of peace

Only unease

Depression

I drink my way

To numbness

Let's have another round

I fuck my way

To connection

Love

Unsuccessfully

Throw another condom on

Nameless stranger on the list

Mediocrity

No energy

No effort

No hope

Gray walls

Gray days

Gray thinking

I don't listen to what

They are saying

It's meaningless

Useless

Hope is a four-letter word

Not the kind I like to say

There is none

When your heart

Has dried up

And the winds have blown it away

Closet Full of Pain

Cover up

With oversized

Baggy clothes

To hide my insecurities

With a painted-on smile

And false bravado

Puffing my chest

Loud words

To distract from my lack of confidence

Full of doubts

Uncertainty

Don't know who I am

Scared to find out

What's really in my heart

What if I don't live up to

My own expectations

Demons

My demons have long legs
Continuously chasing after me
Nipping at my heels
And the fringes of my mind
No matter how hard I hide
They always find me
These demons are large and small
Craving attention
Because I have never acknowledged them
Perhaps all they want is love
Perhaps if I bring them into the light
Of my everyday life
They will no longer be so scary
And less grumpy when I encounter them
All any of us really want
Is connection and love
Even our personal demons

Crown of Pain

You carry your burdens
In your eyes
And in the creases of your heart
Causing it to hurt
Too much
You wear this pain
Like a crown
But you can take it off
You don't have to be
The king of despair

Fear

Oh, Fear, my longtime companion
You had to step up
Step in
Learn to protect the scared child
To stand guard
To keep me safe
You have done your duty well
Blaming others for my shortcomings
Manipulating circumstances and people
To get what was wanted
Creating great anger toward the world
To mask the pain
You were the pilot
Navigating my life
Trolling the shallows of emotions
Never their depths
Avoiding all the challenges, goals, and growth
Numbing the heartache and pain
With drink and drug
I am sorry, my Fear
For leaving you to stand alone
I am here now, to be at your side
I love you, my Fear
For we are one and the same
Take my hand as we walk this life together as one

A dream

Is only hope

With no action

A nightmare

Is hope abandoned

In every action

Part II: Spark

A Dawning Arises

Addiction

Addiction
My old companion
How long have we shared this life
Long enough
That I could not remember
Any other sweet touch
Other than yours
I do recall the pain and suffering
Caused by your numbing embrace
By my using you
To hide my disgrace
Drink drink drink
Glass after glass after glass
I do not hate you though

You tried your best
To protect me
To stave off all that I could not be
When I wouldn't open my eyes
When I was weak
Now! The tables have turned!
I am awakened!
I am empowered!
By self, by love, by love of myself
It's your turn to rest
Your turn to sleep
I will keep watch
I will keep us at peace

Run

I just want to run
From these feelings
From how I feel
Confronting them
Will be hard
Understanding them
Harder
Admitting I might be wrong
The hardest
I just want to hide
From the discomfort
Storming through my stomach
Hide from being uncomfortable
With it all
With them
With myself
But....

But I know
I'm not a coward
Despite being scared
Of emotion
Of the transparency needed
To stop the turmoil
The anguish
The sadness
I'll push through
I always do
Eventually
Deep breaths
Now is the time
Begin
This is how I feel....

Dark Creatures

This is for the dark creatures
That hide in dark places
The shade within us
Gnashing their teeth
Howling
Screaming
Craving attention
Needing to be seen
Scratching
Clawing
At our hearts
Our souls
Our psyche
Wanting to get out
To see the light
To be acknowledged
Loved
Do not abandon these dark creatures
Stop ignoring them
They are a part of us
A part that had to do
The dirty things
The awful, the unspeakable, the bad
So we,
In the light
Could survive
Make sense of our actions
Other's actions
The obscene in the world
Pull those creatures into the fold
Hold them close
Bring the light to them
Thank them
Love them
For they are you
To love
Yourself and others
To be loved
You must love the dark creatures too
Feed them kindness
Know them
They are less scary
When you look at them
Tuck them in
For a long winter's nap
With stories of your healing
Your life
Creating the shade needed
For the heat of existence
Between your light
Their darkness
A union of creatures
Blended
Light and dark

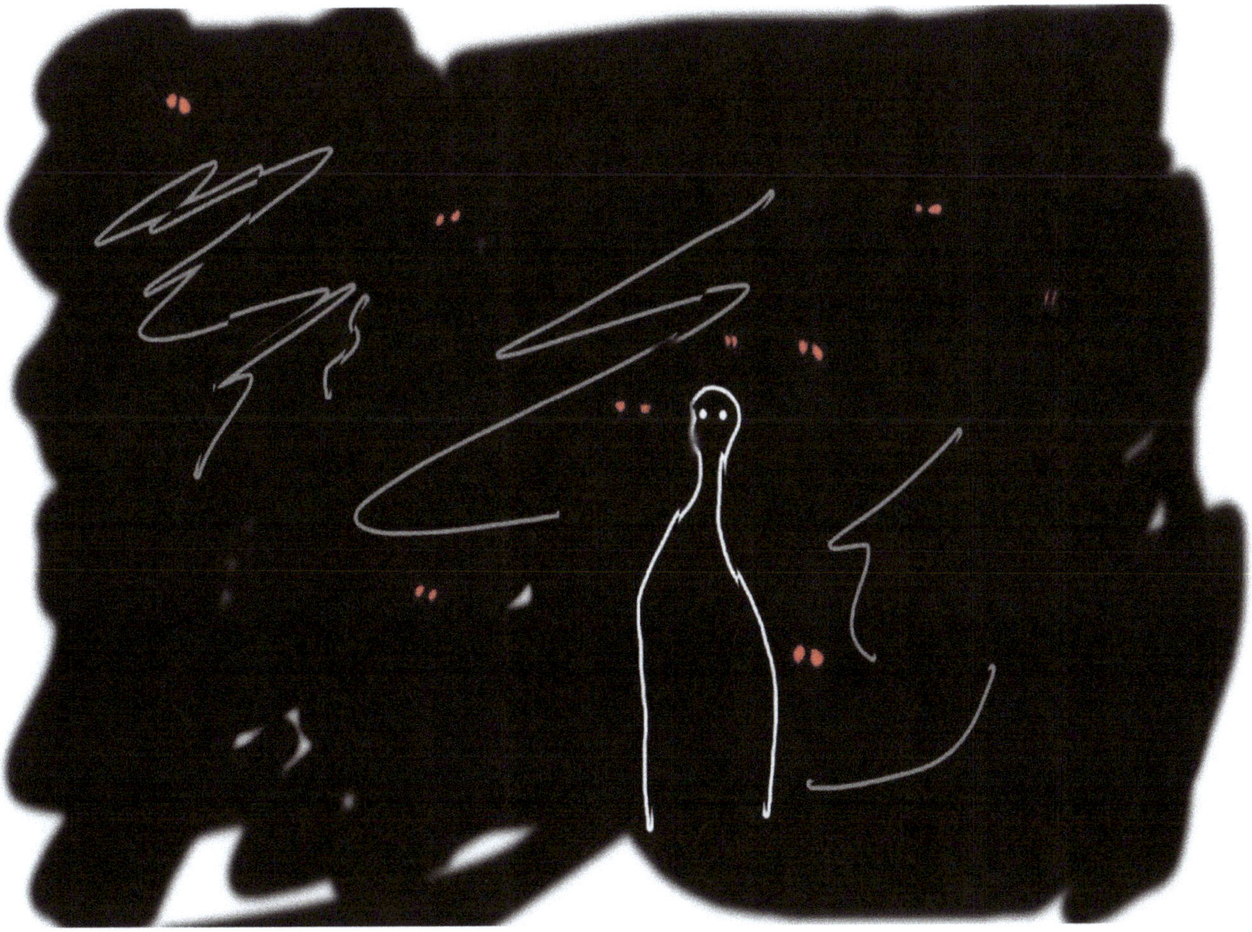

Scars

Underneath these scars

That can't be seen

Lie the secrets

Of my life

Hidden truths

The pain of loss

Heartbreak

Self-hate

Doubt

Run your fingers

Over these invisible

Jagged lines

Kiss them

Love them

Memorize each

And every one

To know them

Is to know me

Help

Do you mind
If I transfer some of this weight
Onto you
It's getting too heavy
To carry alone
The burden
Just a little too much
Right now
Could you take a little bit
Right now
A section of the heaviest part
Give me a second
To catch my breath
I guess what I'm asking is
Can you carry a portion of all my pain
Suffering
Self-doubt
Before I'm crushed under the weight
What I really am asking for
Is your help
Secretly pleading for a hand
It's not easy to do
Admit weakness
Especially in front of you
But help
I won't make it on my own

Cracks

We all have cracks
One way or another
Like a crack in a windshield
It's not pretty
It might let some of the outside world in
But you can still see through it
You're functional
Or cracks in a sidewalk
It might have cracked from the pressure
But you can still play hopscotch on it
Or ride your bike
It can still lead you to where you're going
A crack in your facade
From someone getting close
Making you feel
Letting butterflies escape your carefully
Constructed cage
Yet you still can pull it back together
If needed
Sometimes these cracks make us better
At least vary from the norm
Let us see different
Walk our path differently
Spark growth
Live in the refraction
Cracks aren't always bad
Sometimes they're the most beautiful
Mistakes ever made

Betrayal

There is no worse betrayal
Than the betrayal of self
Not supporting yourself
Loving yourself
Giving yourself the grace
To be human
You give and give to others
But what happens
When your cup has run dry
You have nothing left to give
To anyone
Let alone caring for yourself
Extend to yourself first
What you extend to the world
Patience
Care
Understanding
Forgiveness
You deserve all this and more also
Fill your life first
With all that you want to give
When your container is overflowing
Are you able to pour into the world
Stop the betrayal
Of self

BBB

I'm baffled and bewildered

By the behavior

Of my other self

The irrelevant inconsiderate

Inconsistencies that are selfish

And one-sided

Who is that

Why does he come out

What causes me to switch

How I act

A demon

A derelict

Despite these modes of operation

I think I'm basically good

A person who cares

Personified by giving

How can I merge these two

Mend the split divide

Try try try again

Impetus

Pain

Fear

Addiction

Doubt

Hate

The impetus

For this cathartic pen

Oxidized

I'm tarnished

And oxidized

Weather-beaten

By life

Events

Sometimes it feels

Unrecoverable

But aren't I such a pretty shade

There's no other color

Such as me

Pieces

It's been a long dark night
My life
An example of suppressed emotions
And unfiltered rage
I hemorrhage pain
And unshed tears
My face the picture of a joker
Hysterically laughing
At the mockery this existence has been
All until I came upon you, my friend
Peace
Peace of mind
Acceptance
Of me
My imperfections
Quirks
No longer hating
The flawed image I see
Staring back at me in the mirror
Each moment no longer feeling
Like I walk barefoot
On a path of broken glass
Now realizing I can walk a different road
Or at the least
Protect myself from the jagged
Sharp people
Environments
That cut my soul to pieces
That choice is an option
The option of self
Of love
Of dreams
Instead of nightmares
Stitching my pain with care
And confidence
Sutures made of awareness
Healing ointments of consistency
And effort
Leaving beautiful scars
Unique to just me
Mine to own
All leading from a dark night
Into a slowly dawning new day
Where hope flavors my life
And joy colors the skies
Between the patches
Of dark
Bringing this life
My life
Whole
Uniting the fragmented pieces

Bare

I stand before you
My heart bare
Naked
Vulnerable to my core
This is me
The unfiltered
Undiluted
Pure essence of my being
Accept it
Or don't
My hopes are
That you do
Accept me
Love me
At my rawest
My most honest
But if you do not
I will not change
This is me
In my simplest
Most complex form
Changing
Evolving
But the same at my center
In my Soul
I still fear rejection
I'm not that evolved
But still
Here I stand
Like me or don't
Love me or don't
I'll still have me
Here I stand
True
Tall
All I feel
For you to see
This is Me
Laid bare

Poetry

I am poetry

I'm uncertain when it happened

When there was the anger

Drama

All the insecurities

Victim dialogue I used

The low vibe

Lack

Unelevated version of me

Who didn't know what he didn't know

Or when I began to heal

Starting believing I was human

That mistakes are lessons

That life is good and bad moments

And that's okay

The version of me

That is beginning to understand

It's about the journey

Rather than the destination

I suppose it doesn't matter

I've always been poetry

Just different genres

I have always been poetry

And always will be

Shore

Too far from the shore
Lost sight of the reasons
The purpose
We all have
Adrift in the chaos
Ready to drill holes
In my own boat
Stop!
Stay afloat
Despite the seemingly
Loss of direction
All it takes
Is one lighthouse
One voice
To bring us back to the dock
Back to center
Back to ourselves
When all seems lost
Even yourself
Hold onto that lifeline
No matter how thin
That line runs
The lifeline of hope

Some day
Some how
Some way
There'll be a hand
A word
An act
That will change everything
For you
In you
Hold out
Hold on
Love yourself enough
To hope
Believe
Starting now...

Leaking

What is this
On my cheeks
Leaking from my eyes
What else could I call it
It wasn't intentional
These tears
This bout of crying
I've held it in for so long
Not knowing how or what
To do with them
These emotions
The feelings
From a lifetime
Of suppressed grief
Rage
Emotional neglect
I was never shown
How to express
Never told being me
Was okay
That I was good enough
As I was
Walls built
Always the lingering doubts
Shame
Guilt
A framework for failure
Built-in

Of course it wells up
Escapes at times unexpected
It's okay
It will be okay
I'm learning
Stopping the curse
Generational passing of terrible
Destructive behaviors
I'll stop passing it on
And talk about what I already have
Equip my children
Loved ones
With knowledge I never had
It's okay
To cry
To feel
To fall and fail
It's all normal
It's glorious to be you
To be human
Cry, feel, love fully
Yourself first
Then the world
Let it out
Be you
There's nothing more beautiful
Than you

The Mountain

The mountain

Isn't going to come to you

As much as you

Wish it true

It won't happen

But think

Of all the things you'll learn

Along the way

To that mountain

You see in the distance

Haunted

I'm haunted

By a specter

A ghost

Of who I used to be

Decisions

Influenced by glasses

Overflowing with vodka

Alcoholism

Created by

Conditional love

Self-hate

And Doubt

Rage

Constant Anger

Always present

Always simmering

Just below my skin

Fueled by inner demons

A dark

I was too scared to look at

Back Then

My past still grips my heart

Until I reconcile

Until I accept

All my sides

All the shades

I'll always be haunted

Disciplined

I am not a very disciplined man

I am chaos and blood

I am rampant and rough

I am the storm

Thunder and lightning

Yet I am also the morning after

I am tender and calm

I am love in the air

And the cold in the stream

I am hugs

And heartstrings pulled

I am everything

And nothing at once

I am the earth beneath our feet

And I am the universe at large

I am fierce and tender

I am a mix of everything

Blended and contained

Beneath the skin of a man

Adrift

Sometimes... sometimes
I become... uncentered... adrift
I'll be good
Walking in this beautiful world
Loving the awe
The wonder
Vibing to my own tune
All is right with my universe
Then
I blink
Just blink
And I'm lost
In a desert
Barren
Alone
Upset, angry, questioning
I'm lost in my thoughts
Burdened
Lost in my mind
Scenarios
Lost in my emotions
Overreacting
It may be for an hour
A day
A few even
And then the desert turns to rain
Pouring
Drenching
So hard I can't see
Drowning in my pain
In my misery
But
It's okay
Okay to be lost
How else can I be found
How else can I find new paths
Appreciate what I have
What I'm looking for
What I didn't know I needed
In the desert
The cactus blooms with beautiful flowers
The rain gives life
We can't live without it
It's okay to get lost
It's okay to feel down
Don't stay there
Walk through
Back to the sun
Back to your peace

Choose

Do you think I'm choosing
To be an addict
Do you think I'm choosing to be sad
Lonely
Or exhausted
Or miserable
No, I'm not
I'm choosing to stand up
To fight this
I'm choosing to feel better
I'm choosing a better life
I'm choosing peace
It takes awareness
And then it takes courage
And time
Repetition
And hard work
Feeling better
Creating new habits and mindsets
Is not for the weak or disinterested
It takes failing
And failing again
Then it takes loving yourself
Knowing it's okay to fall
And having the grace for yourself to fall
Not be perfect every day
I'll walk this road of peaks and valleys
I choose to walk this road
To make me better
Strengthen my resolve
With no end in sight
Only lessons and building blocks
As my companions along the way
I choose change
Discomfort
New perspectives
I choose to grow
To evolve from who I was
To who I can be
I choose me

Spill

Losing my way

Losing my balance

Falling

Falling

I hit my head

On the curb of life

All of me spilling out

For the world to see

It's too late

To scoop me up

Put it all back inside

I'm exposed

Time to change

Heal

Or continue to leak

All that is me

All over everything

Everyone

Elevate my vibration

Higher

Close those wounds

Move past

It's time

My life depends on it

On me

Rise

When you're drowning

Holding your breath

Lungs burning

In that moment

You don't understand

Can't comprehend

All the weight

The rocks and boulders

Of burden

The heaviness you're carrying

It's in your hands

Let go

Let it sink

So you may rise

Setting fire

Stop dousing yourself

In self-doubt

Then setting fire

To that toxicity

Burning all the self-love

And confidence

Out of you

View

We both look out the same window

Seeing different imagery

You see the cliff

Dangerous and close

I see the valley

Beautiful and vast

You stare at the bees

Stingers and buzzing

I gaze at the flowers

Blooming and fragrant

We behold the ocean

You worry over how dark and deep

I notice its surf, soothing with rhythm

The scenes

Each the same

Perceived so different

Tilt your head

Make a change

See the beauty

Choice is your power

Choose your view

We look through the same window

What you see is up to you

No Words

No words for tomorrow
I barely get through today
Let the future
Take care of itself
I need to care for me
I have no words of wisdom
Only the painful lessons
Of experience
And regret
I am not my brother's keeper
No paragon of virtue
I am merely a man
A human
Being
Sometimes to the best of my abilities
Sometimes not

I cling to these moments
Every moment
Like a cliff
Desperately trying to survive
But wanting to let go some days
I have no words for tomorrow
Nor today
No words for this moment
Only feelings
That I cannot translate
And seem inadequately small
To describe
Explain
This existence
Of being

Masks

Mask after mask
After mask
All layered
One after another
Piled on top of each other
Not knowing how I look
Without a mask
Who would I be
Would I even know?
Worse yet
Maybe at the end of the day
I wear the masks
In fear that it's blank
Under them all
No face
No one
Is to be found
Feeling like a trail of periods
With no ending
A question mark
Questioning
Answer less
Faceless
A nobody
With nothing
To offer
Nothing to be
No one
Who is under
The masks
One way to find out
Deep breath
Peel each mask off
One at a time

Slipped

I slipped down the mountain

I've given in to grief

It was my misunderstanding

It was supposed to be brief

I didn't understand this pain

I hid it all deep within

Let it change who I am

much to my disdain

Lost myself in a bottle full of drinks

Hard to face your feelings

If you can't even think

Blacked out was better than what I couldn't face

Eventually all that agony comes to a head

My tears and shame would no longer be denied

There had to be a better life to be led

I opened my eyes hoping it could be found

It took so long but I asked for support

Learned to grieve and feel all I felt

Began to see tragedies in a new light

Not the same old story to report

Walk a different road

If you want to arrive at a different destination

Embrace the weight of the emotional load

Be fully you, it's all you can control

Colors

What color is my love

Red like most

What color is my sorrow

Black as the night

What color is my happy

Yellow like summer

But why limit myself

Why label my moods

My vision

The soul

My colors can mean anything

Any emotion or feeling

My colors can be any shade

Any vibrancy or pale reflection

My colors are me

Stop

End of the story

No more boxes

Color me happy, sad, excited, aroused, repulsed, sorrowful, joyful, melancholy

My colors are the spectrum

My colors are beautiful

I wouldn't have it any other way

Beast

There is a beast in all of us

This beast acts differently

For each person

Some beasts are angry

Mean

Spiteful

Others are wild

Crazy

Wandering

They can be ravenous

Destructive

Yet sensitive

Curious

Most of all

You can't kill it

The beast lives within all

Tame it

Incorporate it

You are the beast

It is you

Be the best of both

Door

Where did that door
Come from
Did it just appear
Out of nowhere
I was standing here
Doing what I normally do
Status quo
Day after day
Of the same
That door
Was never there
Lately, I've been switching it up
Making changes
Expanding my mind
Having alternative perspectives
Being more aware of myself
Triggers and thoughts
Creating new versions of me
Working with my shadows
Maybe the door
Is more than a door
An entrance to a new life
Go through it to new worlds
Elevated mindsets
Perhaps the door was always there
I just couldn't see it yet
Until I was ready
Until my vision came into focus

Evolved

I'm not so evolved

I should give advice

I'm not so evolved

That I can offer direction

I can barely stay on my own path

Let alone help find yours

I can't stay out of my own head

I shouldn't jump into yours

I'm not so evolved

That I don't repeat my own mistakes

I'm not so evolved

To help you avoid your missteps

I float upon my own river

Drifting to an ocean that holds us all

I'm not so evolved

To think I can steer your ship

But I have grown

From where I started

I am more aware

Occasionally observing where I tripped so easily

I'm not so evolved

But I have evolved a bit

Soulfully

Free Like a Bird

I've opened the cage
To all this misery
One of these days, the pain
Has to fly away
I'll heal when it's time
The scars will be beautiful
Until then
I'll bleed the poison
Slowly from my body
And mind
Given my disposition
I won't rush
It's not indecision
I'm just more careful
Than I need to be
It's so hard to trust
The world
And myself
The process
The readiness
The pain will fly like a bird
When it is time

Not to Be

I'll not be
What you want
I'll not
Make myself less
For you
I'll not
Fit in your box
Or play by your rules
It's difficult enough
Piecing myself together
Learning my curve
I will be
Myself
Whomever that is that day
I will be authentic
Until that authenticity
No longer rings true
I'll be me
Through and through
As I figure it out

Opaque

The trappings of my mind

Trip me up

As I walk through life

Thoughts

Worries

Make me stumble and fall

Doubt my path

Decisions

Sometimes I only see myself

Through an opaque lens

Distortion

False images

I pray

To whom I am unsure

That one day

My thoughts will be my own

Friendly

Uplifting

Loving

To myself

Eventually

Consistently being authentically me

Mind, body, and soul

How to Love

I don't know how to love
I searched for so long
Pushed it
Faked it
I gave and gave and gave
But for me
Not for the others
It came with strings
Attachments
Always a conditional
If I do this
You must return that to me
Me me me
How could I love
When I was so selfish
Not with an open heart
But closed
Bitter
Angry
At the world
People
Who were supposedly close to me
Important

How could I know how to love anyone else
When I couldn't love myself
Stand to see the sight
Of my own face
Look at my true self
Ugly
Needy
Wanting
A lost fool
Who couldn't see the truth
Right before him
His mind
His own heart
I don't know how to love
Because I don't even know me
Myself
My heart
Too scared to be honest with the world
Let alone the man in the mirror
Too small to admit fault
All blame
Wallowing in shame

A step from the gallows

But begging for a hand

To pull me back

From the noose of self-hatred

The edge of giving up hope

When all along

It took me

A tired me

A better me

A me that was sick of the bullshit excuses

Uttered from my own mind

The life I allowed to happen

To me

A me to say enough

To ask for help

Guidance

To ask where is the love

And how do I find it

And allow the possibility

Time has passed

And I don't have all the answers

And I fall and I fail and I struggle

And that is beautiful

Because I'm trying

I am moving forward

With open eyes

A humbled ego

And a heart cracking open

New thoughts

Seeking change

Awareness deepening

And more allowance

Of authenticity

Authentically me

I don't know how to love

But I know more today than I did yesterday

I'm learning

I'm crying

I'm evolving

In ways I've never dreamed

And I love it

In Between

I try to learn the lessons
Life is teaching
In the in-between moments
Of the deafening crescendo
Of day-to-day
I let the silence trickle
Into my mind
Reflecting and redefining
Reshaping the mold
Of my lens
Adjusting perspectives
As I grow
As I change
Shedding old traits and habits
That no longer suits today or me
Soaking in knowledge
No longer fighting it
That my skin
My person
My persona
This soul
Will shed and morph and elevate
Time and time and time again

If I'm aware enough
Willing enough
Open enough
Closing those chapters of the story
I didn't write for myself
Staring at blank pages
Pen in hand
Ready to write the stories I want
The true stories
My story
Listening to the in-between moments
Allowing my essence
My heart and soul
To be free
To be me

Shaded

What color is my soul
I'm not sure anymore
What hue was it
When I was born
How has it changed
Through my life
My experiences
Was it a rainbow
At some point
Is it jaded now
Shaded
By your influences
Is it black now
What color is my soul
Honestly, it doesn't matter
The shade, hue, or pigmentation
I just need to know
It's the color it needs to be
For me
Right now
In this moment
Shaded perfectly
Soulfully
Me

Tiny Thoughts

Why do I persist

To make myself small

Put myself in a box

Of my own making

If I ever want to grow

Become who I am meant to be

I have to stop thinking this way

Giving in

To my tiny thoughts

When I'm so much bigger than them

Threadbare

My soul

Is feeling

Threadbare

Worn so many times

Wearing thin

Like a favorite shirt

So comfortable

At ease

At home

My soul

Tried and true

Joyful and old
Wrinkled

Weathered

Wearable
My soul
Threadbare

Rest

I laid to rest
My past
It had simply become
Too heavy
Then I closed my eyes
To the future
I keep looking there
Instead of all around me
I had to stand in the present
It was slipping by
Without me realizing
All my wasteful days I wasn't using
Leading to unhappiness
Not enjoying anything happening to me
While I carried the past
Looking to the future
It finally dawned on me
An epiphany
The world wasn't happening to me
It was all for me
If I just grabbed it
Asked for it and adored it
The good
The bad
And tragedy
All how I choose to see it unfolding
Life was my oyster
Though I don't like the taste
It has given pearls
It's up to me to use the wisdom granted
Fill the cracks with gold
Don't turn my back
Be bold
And let the universe
Take me where we are going
Don't hold on too tight
Just let your energy flow
What's meant to be
Will follow

Unforgiven

You
Are unforgiven
For all that you do to me
For all the pain
You have caused
Why can't you just love me
The way I want to be loved
Why can't you
Love me the way I love you
Unforgiven
For all the years I've begged
For your attention
And been left wanting
You are
Unforgiven
For not making me your priority
Not showing how much
I should mean to you
Making me sad and lonely

One day
The mirror said to me
You are the most foolish of fools
You blame your misery
On her
And others
When the only one to blame
Is in this mirror
You yourself are the unforgiven
By yourself
Looking out for all the reasons
When looking in provides
All your answers
You are unforgiven
By self
The first step is to love
And forgive
Yourself

I Don't Know

I didn't know

How to do it

Where to start

I wasn't ready

Unaware

Suffering

Overwhelmed

Suddenly

One day

I decided

I must change

So I did

With effort

With help

Clumsily

It hurt

It still can

It's messy

Change is

Through the chaos

I emerged

Step by step

Day by day

Never perfect

But feeling better

Empowered and brave

Stronger than before

How did I do it?

I just did

I choose to evolve

Not doomed to repeat

Falter

I begin to falter
Cave to the weight of the world
On my shoulders
Still not as heavy as the thoughts
Of my own mind
Crushing my spirit
Weighing each footfall
Until I cannot move
This is life
This is what it is to be human
But this weight
The thoughts
Will not stop me
A deep breath
Then another
A day of rest
Clear my vision
Renew my spirit!
Onward
Upward
I may slow
But I will never stop
Faltering is not losing
Failing
Is but a lesson
Opportunity
I falter
But then I move
Again
And again

The first thing to master

Is yourself

The rest

Will fall into place

In time

Part III: The Journey

Dancing Between the Dark and the Light

A Story

This is a story
Of a small scared boy
Looking for love
Seeking acceptance
Safety
Who grew into a man
A lost man
An angry man
With no coping skills
No trust
No idea how to understand
His feelings
Any emotions
That were not surface-facing
Bumbling through life
Stumbling
Drunken
Sad
Lonely
But this also is a story
Of redemption
Rising
Facing demons
Self
Of walking through
The confusion
Shame
Turning the view
From downcast eyes
Accusing states of mind
Into forward-facing
Self-reflecting gazes
Inward
This is a story of healing
Hurting
And healing more
Accepting there is always healing
Layers to unfold
Never perfect
But healthier
Some days
But happier
Most days
And it's okay
It
And he
Will be all right
Even when sad

Even alone

His smile

Laughter

Will return

This is the story of life

Rejuvenation

Reflection

Realizing it's not the roller coaster

Of a ride

Causing your distress

But your reactions

And lack of self-discipline

To that ride

Where troubles arise

This is a story

About you

Your journey

And how you perceive

React

To it

This is a story

Of the steps

Footfalls

Taken

On the journey

We all get to the end of the story

How you do so

Is your story

Empty Space

What is this empty space
I feel?
It used to be for want
For what I didn't think I had
This space has been for words
I couldn't say
Caught
Too scared
Too dumb
Sitting in that empty space
Until they decay away
It has been for lost love
Forever hollow
Yearning
For that feeling
That won't come back
That empty space
For all the maybes
Maybe I'll do this or that
In the future
Maybe I'll go back to school
Maybe try a new hobby
Stop drinking
Diets
Maybe I will someday
Maybe love will be mine
Wasted space
Now my empty space
Is reserved for me
An empty space for me
To grow
Emotionally
Spiritually
Intellectually
I hold this empty space
For present Scott
To grow into future Scott
Each day
Each moment
Even in the times
I don't
I hold space for me

Home

Crying
Tears coming like glass
A trail of blood
Across my cheeks
The wilderness is harsh
And I've been lost for so long
My mind has unraveled
My body beaten
My soul discolored
Exhausted as the night
Just before dawn
Barely hanging on
I had fallen
But was not out
Inch by inch
Thought by thought
I'm recovering myself
Fighting for my real self
On one knee
Then on my feet
Face to the sun
No more shame

No more outside
Influence
Expectations
I'd wandered far from my center
Who I am
But now
I'm coming home
I'm coming home
I'm coming home
Crawling
Walking
Running
Back home
Home
To who I really am
Was meant to be
All along
Home to
Authentic me
Smile again
You can find
Your true home

Flow

Why do you fight it???
With all your might
Like it was a beast
Or a monster
Like it was there to hurt you
Cause you pain
It's called life, but...
You take it personal
An attack just on you
Like you are the universe
The center of it all
Let go
You can't control
The situation, the result
The good, the bad
Don't try, let it go
You can't control
Other people, events, much of it all
Stop, stop trying
You are hurting yourself
None of those are about you
You are about you
Master you
That's your control
Let go
Be like water
Flow
Around the rocks
Down the falls
Traverse the world
Watch it all as it goes by
Enjoy, experience, exalt
Let your life be like water
And let it flow

So Close

I felt so close

To a breakthrough

To making progress

Climbing closer

To the summit

Reaching the shore

Of self-love

Peace

But now

The under tow

Of self-doubt

Self-hatred

Drags me under

To the dark

The depths of my mind

Drowning in worthlessness

I've fallen off the cliff

Of that mountain

Into an abyss

Of self-pity

Loathing

The light gone from both places

I'd gone so far

Only to recede

Regression

Left empty

Be Grateful

Be grateful?
For this pain that will not go away
For this darkness
That will not incorporate into my light
For this shit that I shovel out of my hole
Only to be filled with my tears
That eventually drown me
Slowly
Inescapably
Be grateful?
That all the work I've done
On me
My inner child
On that void
Which swallows all progress
Joy
Happiness
Disappears in the blink of an eye
I suppose
I'm grateful I keep trying
I'm grateful
I realize these things are happening
And I'm not living in ignorance of it
Anymore

I'm grateful I don't quit
That I always take a step
Even if it's a half-step
Or after I've been knocked back three steps
I still move forward
I'm grateful
For those that see the good in me
And accept the not so good
I'm grateful I'm eventually able to laugh
Shake off the shackles of seriousness
And know
Even if it's in the back of my mind
This life
This journey
This path
Is winding
Full of smooth and rough
Up and down
Everything and nothing
So yes
I am grateful
Even if it's not every moment of every day

Control

Do you know

What it takes

To keep the wolves at bay

Their snarling and biting

At your heels

Foaming at the mouth

Vicious

Their whole pack circling

Ready to strike

Me

Standing alone

Tall

I cannot control the pack

Their intentions

Their bark or bite

All I can do

Is control me

My emotions and reactions

Ignore the bark

And carry a big stick for

The bite

Drank

I drank
And drank
And drank
And drown most days
On emotions
On self-loathing
On misunderstanding
On pain
On the dark hateful places within me
On the fucking stories others wrote for me
That I believed
That I thought were written in stone
Alcohol was just the vehicle
The tool to self-destruct
To keep myself trapped
Scared
To not believe
In myself
My heart
My capabilities
Putting the glass down
Ending my choice of poison
Was the start
To my story
That I write
The world I make
To truly walk my walk
My path
Who knows where it will go
But I get to navigate now
I choose
Good
Bad
Endless possibilities
I drank and drank fear and loathing
Guzzled self-pity
For so long
I now sip on hope
Love
My power
It's sweet
And sometimes sour
But I fill the cup now
With my choice of
What's in the chalice of my life
I drank before
Now I float
On the optimism
Of what I am creating
I'll drink to that

Broken Mirrors

I love broken mirrors

They make me feel at home

Fractured

Jagged

Their reflection is truly

My own

So many pieces

Innumerable refractions

Just like my mind

Exposing its countless sides

Changing moods

And unexplainable reactions

I love broken mirrors

They expose my true reflection

My inner me

Allowing everyone

To see what I see

Golden Road

For so long
I've looked for
The yellow brick road
To deliver me
Where I've wanted to go
No more
I've stopped
I'll just walk
On whatever is in front of me
Grass
Cement
A dirt path
Or trepidation
It doesn't matter
Taking the first step
Is what's important
The destination
Is only the where
It's the why
That makes the reason
It's the how
That makes us change
Who cares
If the road is golden
As long as there's love and growth
Every step is worth
The pleasure and pain
One foot after another
Stumble and fall
Rest and run
Be open
To where it takes you
Love yourself
And love the way
In a golden glow

Anchors

I will no longer
Chain myself
To the anchors
Of expectations
Mine
Yours
Or the world's
I will rise like a balloon
Free from a hand
Or a wave
Surfing the ocean
Both free
To go where the breeze pleases
Or the tide pulls you
There is a life
That is going to happen
No matter your choices
Learn to enjoy the flow
Where it takes you
Instead of being
Battered and bruised
By the currents and winds
When you are fighting
The whole way
When you're stuck in place
Let go
This is when the true journey
Is the beginning

Caterpillar

Dried butterfly wings
And caterpillar tears
Over the fear of change
Never approached the chasm
The abyss of the unknown
Shall always be black
All that could
Shall never be
No metamorphosis
No cocoon
Forever stagnant
Stuck walking
When bravery
Could have flown you there
On wings of possibility

Cry

I've always felt tears

A moment's notice away

Welling, waiting, flowing

Stop! Hold them back!

You're no man, they say

Why do I feel this way

Am I wrong?

Am I flawed?

Why must I hide

These emotions, these feelings, this love

The gazing judgment of the world

Lingers heavily upon my mind

More tears, more pain, confused and drained

Ego bruised; confidence fractured

How should this go????

I am just a man, I don't know....

But... with every new day

There is a dawning, an awakening

A choice to learn

These tears, they are mine

Treasures of my soul

Gifts from my heart

Of love, of pain, of joy, of heartache

For no reason!

I rejoice in you!

In each teardrop, in each heavy sigh

They are every part of me

Not to be shamed but celebrated, acknowledged, accepted, allowed

I am man, I am human, I am flawed

Cry, Scott, cry

Alone in Bed

Do you ever
Sit in bed
Alone
And wonder
How did this all happen
How did I end up here
Was it all my choices
Not that it's bad
Not that it's not another's dream
But it might not be yours
Not what you envisioned
How life would go
Are you sad?
Disappointed?
Or just
Okay?
Not excited
Enthused
Should you just be grateful
For what you have
Though it's not what you wanted
Or exactly how you wanted
Restart?
The answer alludes me
Sometimes the path too
I'm not really alone
I have me
That should be enough
I need to remember that
But I don't
And the way is difficult
When I think too much
Or have certain expectations
Another day
Another try
Another me when the time is right
Until then
Laughter
Tears
And all that I have to give

@HOPE.TIAN

Corners

I keep hoping
Around the next corner
I'll find a better life
I'll be happier
If I keep walking
And turn the next corner
I'll be a different person
Better than now
How do I find
What I'm looking for
I keep moving
Looking for that next corner
To turn
But each time
I find the same old problems
Nothing changes
Same old me
Maybe that's why
Around every corner
The scenery looks familiar
New places
Does not mean new behaviors
It's time to stop
Stop looking for corners to turn
To change my life around
All I want
Is inside me
This soul
This heart
Is where it starts
And the shadowy corners
Of my mind
Stop running
Face me
And here is where
I'll find my home
I've been looking for
Around those corners

Head

If I could crack open this head
Dig through this mind
Pick out the thoughts that hurt me
The negative self-talk
The feelings of worthlessness
The judgements
Of me
Others
I'd perform that surgery
I'd cut them out
Bleed down my face
Into my eyes
Over my hands
I'd scream from the pain
And do it again and again
Because it couldn't hurt more
Than I already do
Have
For all these years
All this time
The bad things swirling around this brain
Have cut deeper
Than any physical pain
I've ever endured
Would it do any good
Would I feel any better
I don't know
But it has to be better
Then continuing on
The same

Eyes Open

Dreams drip from my eyelids

I try to glue them shut

To keep these hopes alive

Inside of me

But in the end

I realized

Dreams are better

When you're awake

Always there to see

Remember vividly

Eyes wide open

To experience every drop

Of the pain and pleasure

As you chase

And catch those dreams

They turn to memories

You have them

Your whole life

Let it all play out

Day and night

I'll keep reaching

And dreaming

As if

It's my life's right

Dust

My old self

An outdated version of me

Is gone

Disintegrated

But I sit in the same space

Breathing in the dust of

My former selves

It's time to move on

And up

Leave the dust

The past

Behind

Take in the new

Breathe the now

Deep

Cleansing

Breathes

Opening dimensions

Portals

To anywhere

Any way

I want to grow

Air as sweet as possibilities

Emotional

I can feel them

Lurking

Waiting

Bubbling

Near the surface

Wanting to be free

Surging

No! No, you can't

Stay down, stay away

What will I do with you

How will I react

They come with pain

No more, no more pain

Brought on

By the simplest thing

A word, a note, a look, a lyric

It doesn't take much

So many tears

Why does it have to be bad

Isn't it normal

To feel, to be

Emotional

It's a part of life

A way through

To another side

A walk through the pain

A different view

To a healthy place

Safe

Comfortable

A mix, all facets of me

Made whole

Just by being

Emotional

Feel

If I could cry for you
I would
If I could feel for you
The way I should
The way you deserve
I would
But the past and the lies
I told myself
And believed from the world
Caged my emotions
Locked my true self away
I hope you see the glimpses
Of my heart
Of me
I'll work for you
For us
But mostly for me
To be free
To release all this
Stuck inside of me
Before I burst
Before I die
This is what I want
This is who I want to be
I want to love
I want to feel
I need to experience
The rainbow
The spectrum of all that I can be
All that I can feel
There'll come a time
I'll cry for you
And for me
And everything between

Choice

I stand on the shores of life
Afraid of the ocean
It's unknown depths
The unseen
Yet afraid of the sands of stagnation also
Swallowing me
Anchored in a perpetual state of static
Unchanged
Which fear is greater
The unknown
Or the unevolved
Movement or standing still
Possibilities of tomorrow
Whatever they may be
Or the known of the now
And the stories of the past
It's a choice
Your choice
What will you choose
Who will you be

Belief

I reached a spot
In my journey
A realization
I've always thought
I'm not good enough
For anything
Smart
Worthy
Looking
Believed that I lacked confidence
And that is where the real menace lies
Belief
Or lack of
I don't believe in me
Or didn't
With what I've done
Accomplished
Opportunities grabbed
Chances taken
Mistakes made
Falls taken
Phoenix moments gloriously
If unceremoniously had
The small
The big
The in between
Moments
All taken
All lived
Poorly or well
I did it
The proof is in the living
The deeds
The actions
I always thought
I was resilient
And I am
But I'm confident as hell
I just didn't believe it
Until now
What I really am
Is fucking magical
There's only one me
I'm scarred
Beaten
Bruised
Tough
Smart

Learned

Ignorant

Scared

Brave

Kind

Thoughtful

Selfish

Mean

I am authentic

I am humorous

I am confidence

And it is all beautiful

This is my fuck yeah poem

Fuck yeah, I believe

In me

Though doubt might creep back

Sometimes

Some days

It's too late

I know

Now

I am belief

In me

Fuck yeah, me

Breathe

I breathe

In this day

This moment

I expand

In mind

Feelings

My heart exploding

With love

As my lungs fill

With the wonder

Of this world

As my thoughts

Untangle from the hectic

Mundane

Freeing from expectation

And judgements

Fear

I breathe

All that there is

That can be

Breathe

Where there is breath

there is hope

Where there is life

there is hope

Where there is resilience

there is hope

And where there is understanding of self

there can be the beginning of peace

Part IV: Hopeful

A Genesis of Understanding and Peace

Crutch

I've used a crutch my whole life

And sometimes

It's okay

When you're hurting so deep

So deep inside

That you just can't

Work

Talk

Function

But when you're feeling better

Healing

Healed

You need to stand on your own

Walk on your own two feet

Lean into your heart

Let all the crutches go

The excuses

Accept or change

Walk through that pain

While feeling the pain

With each step

Becoming stronger

With each footfall

The waste

The blame

Falls aside

Then one day

You realize

You don't need those crutches

Anymore

Knight

I am no white knight

In shining armor

I am no prince

Nor king upon a throne

I am merely me

Discovering who that is

As time passes on

It is up to others

To assign titles or names

To cast judgments

Or assumptions

I am simply me

Moment to moment

Day after day

Ribbons

I spun apart

Like ribbon from a spool

I had to come undone

In order to be remade

Spun back together

But in a new form

A similar shape

Appearance

Yet completely different

New experiences

To be had

New views for new eyes

In the same shade of blue

New learning

More lessons

Until the time

To spin again

Ribbons unfurling

Making room

More lives to create

Many versions of me

In this lifetime

Shine

I'm so blind
I don't even see my own shine
I should
But I put blinders on
To hide from my grand design
Others try to tell me
Of how much
I do shine
But I make excuses
Of why the gleam is tarnished
In my own eyes
Dimmed through the lens of disdain
They try to show me
Of the glow of my shine
From the inside
How I care for others
Always willing to lend a hand
Or offer a word of encouragement
I brush it off
In the form of humble deflection
But it's time for that to stop
Put my doubts in their place
And let out
What I know has always been there
Inside my heart, down to my soul
The sun, a nova, the brightest star
In my sky
It's time to let this light shine
My self shine
Authentically unapologetically
Me
Shine through my smile
Through my actions
Through my heart
A shine that's just mine

Grateful

I've never been grateful
I've always wanted more
Situations
People
Life
Have never lived up to
The imagination in my head
Always focused on the past
Or the future
On the what I don't have
Instead of what's here
In front of me
The moment
But a veil is lifting
A shift in thought
I'm beginning to see
What's really here
What is important
To me
What matters most
To my world
I hope it's not too late
Let me continue to learn
Gratitude

Let me be grateful
For the joy I have
The treasures I did not
Open my eyes to
It wasn't buried
I was looking
Searching
In the wrong places
I was holding the map
Upside down
Turn it
A fresh perspective
A different angle
Of the same picture
Brings new views and sights
All worthy
All to be grateful for
Don't let it be too late
Before my vision clears more
And I realize how wealthy
I truly am
How much I have to be
Grateful for

Constraints

I'm going take to this paper

Till the ink runs dry

And the well of my emotions

Runs empty

This paper

Will feel everything I can't

Weep

Laugh

It will take the shape of love

And be ripped into a thousand pieces

Of heartbreak

I no longer need to suppress

Only express

From my heart

This soul

All that I feel

To be free

Of past constraints

And be all that I am

Black Tar

This black tar

Running through my veins

Poisoning my mind

Poisoning my life

Fueled by hate

Pumped by fear

How do I turn this tar

Into blood

How do I thin it down to love

I no longer want this sludge

Slowing me down

This drudgery

Bringing me to heel

Lowering my vibration

This sticky pine tar

Keeping me stuck

Is over

From stuck to free

Heel to heart

Low to heavenly

Hopeless to hopeful

From tar to gold

Canvas

Life is a canvas

You the artist

How you live

The art

You don't need to be Picasso

Or Van Gogh

Art is subjective

And the only opinion that matters

Is yours

So paint away

Be wild

Imaginative

Or calm

And subdued

It's your canvas

Your life

Just paint

As much as possible

As often as you can

Enjoy the process

And fill every bit of canvas

You can

Fire

The air is on fire

But it doesn't burn me

It fills my lungs

Ignites my heart

And dissolves the lies from my tongue

Cleaning my spirit

Clearing my path

It reflects the spark in my eye

And breathes life into possibilities

This fire is hope

Love

This fire is me

Awake

I'm awake now

But it still feels like a dream

This new world

That has opened to me

I never want to sleep again

If it means

Going back to where I used to be

Let the waking hours

Merge with the dreaming

Powering my true self

Eyes continuing to remain open

New thoughts

New perspectives

New experiences

Leading to a new version of me

The struggle is real

But the work

Is worth the prize

YOU

Life is Life

Here's some things
I've learned the hard way
Life is life
Life is the whole thing
Sometimes you'll cry your eyes out
Sometimes you'll laugh your brains out
Boring and mundane
Exciting and thrilling
A roller coaster
Peaks and valleys
The dark and the light
The constant is you
You're experiencing your life
Feel happy
Feel sad
Just feel
In the moment
Be the moment
Then walk through it
To the next moment
And the next and the next
What I've learned is
You have the power over you
Not life
Not the moments
But how you handle the moment
Or not
We aren't always going to do well
Learn from it
Do better
Or don't
That is your power
Harness it
Live
Then live more
Enjoy
Experience
Ride the waves
That life is
Be grateful
For you can choose how you
experience life
That's your power
Be a superhero
Or a victim
You choose

Occasionally

It happens occasionally

A calmness

Falls over me

At peace

With myself

The world around me

Patchwork

My life is a patchwork

I am a patchwork

Of my experiences

My traumas

My loves

I am made up of everything

That has happened to me

Happiness

Sadness

Joy

Terror

Tumbled together

But I get to determine

How they are stitched together

I choose the pattern

Aren't I beautiful?

Heavy

It's heavy

Because you carry it

Day after day

Year after year

Hold it in the moment

Then let it go

The weight will be gone

Carry the lesson

It's lighter

And more valuable

Not the weight

Of judging yourself

Damaged Goods

Damaged goods
That's what I am
But listen
To the words
Damaged not broken
Goods
I'm good
I still work
Pretty damn well, too
Not perfect
Personality quirks
I may have a dent or two
Here and there
A scar
These are just lessons
Character
I wouldn't trade my damaged goods
For perfection
Shiny or new
Any day of the week
It's what makes me
Me
Awesomely me
I'm damaged goods
And damn proud of it

Feel

Can you feel it?

Peace

Calm

Emerging from the storm

By not fighting it

No longer raging

Against the swirl

Letting go

Flow

Accepting the rain

The thunder

Turmoil

Knowing

What's coming next

The sun

Shining as bright

As the storm was loud

Accepting

All will be right

Eventually

A breeze soothes your soul

A smile warms your heart

You are at peace

There is calm

In the eye of your storm

Attention

I tried talking to the sky
But it feigned ignorance
To my lies
I attempted to buy the ocean
A drink
But she said her thirst
Had been quenched
When Moses parted the Red Sea
I smiled at the sun
But was ignored
Apparently it has eyes
Only for the moon
I begged the moon, then,
To think only of me
But she said
I am for all to see
I looked in the mirror
And found
This is truly
Where my attention needs to be
If I start with self
Be honest and nurture
Love the child within
Then it will not matter anymore
What I sought without

Groove

I'm findin' my groove

Getting in tune

With the being

Beneath this skin

With who I am

Dancing into my soul

Envy

I envy the sky
For its openness
I envy the wind
Enjoying its freedom
I envy the stars
With their twinkling
I envy the world
In all its beauty
Then I realized
I am beautiful
In all my flawed glory
I am as bright
As any star twinkling
I am as free
As I choose to be
And I am as authentic as the sky
When I allow my humanity free
I am the universe
I am all things
I no longer envy
Anything
I live

Limitless

An ocean in a little white box
I don't know if there's anything sadder
A waterfall stranded in the desert
Maybe there is that
There are so many things in this world
Not being what they are
Not doing what they were meant to
Don't find yourself
Being one
So stretch your legs
And expand your mind
Leave fear at the door
As you enter this whole new world
The world of possible
The days of why not
So spread your wings and fly
Like you were meant to
A never-ending sky
Be that waterfall
In the jungle
Be the ocean
Covering all the worlds
Limitless
Just like you
If you allow
If you
Welcome it

Your

Your truth

Your self

Your authentic self

Has been bought

And paid for

By your hard work

Your shadow work

Your determination

For growth

For spiritual learning

For not quitting

When you wanted to

For finding your worth

At the bottom of that well

Of emotions

And pain

Cash that damn check

You've earned it

Wear your peace

Your happiness

That beautiful soul

A genuine smile

You paid your price

Now enjoy it

Numb

I remember being numb
To life
To adversity
The slightest twinge of pain
Drown that shit
Kill it with booze
Emotionally stunted
Spiritually deadened
Asleep to life
As bleak as the dark side of the moon
It took me so long
To realize
There are stars
On that side of the moon too
I just couldn't see them
From my perspective
In that time
Perspectives change
Shift
And light can enter all places
Mingle and merge
With the dark
You can grow
Emotions come under control
Life blooms
The spirit can awaken
Sometimes
Sometimes I still want to feel numb
To not be hurt
For it all
To be easy
But that's not change
Not Real
Not Living
Growth of self
Awareness
Possibilities
Has taught me
To see the light and the dark
You miss so much
Without the embrace
Of the feelings
Of all your feelings
They make up
All of you

Shadow

I stand in the shadow
Of my own greatness
Believing it is cast
By the monolith
Of other people's power
The reality is
It's my power
Given away
By fear of judgment
And achievement
What I'm really capable of
If I tried
Life lived without reservation
This shadow is my greatness
Should I step into it
Eclipsing my fear

Is

There was no right answer
There is no perfect
But there is beauty
In acknowledging
Trying
Working toward improvement
Even small
Incremental
Do not be discouraged
By the slide
It's inevitable
Remember
No perfection
We are human
Flawed
Broken
But those cracks
Crevices
Allow the world in
Change
Experiences
And our inner shine out
For our own magic
To seep into others
Spread
There is no right answer
There is effort
There is
What there is
And what you make of that

Horizons

Horizons

Are like faith

You can't see it

But you know it's out there

Somewhere

Just out of reach

But an event

Coming up quick

I look forward to my horizons

Who knows what they'll bring

Each one a surprise

Or a lesson

Point your north to that horizon

And keep going

You'll never get anywhere

If you don't

The Thing

Here's the thing
It's tough
Stuff
People
Life
No one ever guaranteed
It would be easy
Here's the more important thing
So are you
Tough
Strong
Resilient
Way more than you think
Take a breath
Pause a moment
A million moments
If you need
Smile
Then take your next step
You can
At your own
Pace

Ghosts

I'm surrounded by ghosts
Remnants of souls
I've known and loved
Echoes of feelings
Seen in my mind
Down to my heart
Shades flickering
With each beat
Every breath
Haunting
My waking and sleeping hours
Shambling
Floating past me
Near me
In between blinks
Screaming ghouls of
Unreleased pain
Stored grief
Begging to be set free
Breathe them in
Through my heart
Beyond this corporeal form
And back out
Through my heart
To be loved
Told goodbye
And freed to the mists of the
past
Tears allowed
The first in years
Sobbing
Violently to a soft moan
With relief
Full of love
These wraiths
Back to where they belong
And me
Restored to myself
A true form
No longer a shell of who I could
be
No longer a ghost myself
That I couldn't see
Through the stored emotional
specters
That I held to close
But could not let go of
I learned to walk through and
away
From them
No more ghosts

Foundation

Take this uncertainty
From my skin
My mind
Ignite it
With the heat of pursuit
The focus of intention
The desire to elevate
The man
Person
Human being
I am today
Into a better version tomorrow
Melt this doubt
Like wax as a candle burns
Illuminating my vision
Clearing shadows
Creating a path
To follow
For many tomorrows to come
Let me pour confidence
Boundaries
Esteem
Self-love
Into the foundation
The future
My future
My children's future
Can be set upon

A Dream Within a Dream

I remember

Only slightly

Through a drunken haze

Every day

Every night

All the life I tried to avoid

A dream within a dream

But more like a nightmare

I remember

Vividly

All the feelings

And shoving them down

Not knowing how to navigate through

I didn't have the tools

Or knowledge

Of what to do

Or how to understand them

A dream becoming a nightmare

I remember

Watching my life

From the outside

Peering in through a window

Like a voyeur

Or a creep

I stopped being present

For my family and me

Alcohol and drugs numbing my being

Only a nightmare remained

I remember

The moment

When I wanted it to stop

Embarrassed

And not knowing who I was anymore

What happened to the funny and loving man

I used to be

I had to make a change

There was no one else to blame

Time to end the nightmare

I remember

Reaching out

Help

Help me

I'm drowning in all that I am

It took strength and tears

Walking through my pain

Learning the truth

All over again

The truth of who I am

Not my deeds or stories I believed

It taking time and intention

Love for self

And belief

I've stripped away all the excuses

Looked in the mirror

And know now

It's all up to me

But I'm not alone

And I cry freely

Feeling all that I am

And letting it go

I remember

I'm not perfect

And that's okay

Forgiving myself

It's time for grace

Looking back now

It all seems

Like a dream within a dream

Choose

Then the days turned into nights
And the nights turned into years
I keep burying all my turmoil and pain
All the unhappiness became disdain
Indifference became the standard
And I didn't know
The reflection in the mirror
Who I was gone
And who I wanted to be was forgotten
Ignoring all
I fell deeper down that hole
All longing lost
All that was left was the job I hated
And a family I barely knew
A tumbler full of vodka and ice
Was all that got me through
But buried me
Further down an emotional abyss
Sinking sinking sinking
Is all I felt
Sad and lonely every day
Feeling sorry for myself
How do you turn it around
How do you initiate change
By force of will
Enough clarity to realize
This is not how you want to live
The bottom is a terrible place to be
But an amazing place to push off from
When or where can you start
Now
Tomorrow
As soon as you can
As you will
All it takes is the power to say
Ready set go
And the perseverance
To walk through the fire of change
Putting the work in
To work on self isn't easy
Chaos isn't easy
But do you prefer just chaos
Or chaos with a purpose?
A better life
A better you
It all comes down to
What do you choose

Give Up

I've given up control I've never really had

Let the winds of change have their way with me

Set adrift in uncertainty and excitement

Feel the tingle of electricity run down my spine

There is no end in sight on this road I travel

What better way to live then to enjoy the journey

And not the destination

Watercolors

I don't want

To live my life

Like it was painted

In watercolors

Vague

Blurry

Out of focus

It's beautiful

In a painting

But not for living

This life

My life

I want to be

Vibrant!

Tuned in

Clear

Intentional

Let me see the world

My goals

My dreams

The present

Every day

Vividly

That doesn't mean

Some days aren't

A beautiful mess

Enjoy those too

On occasion

Those watercolors

Nothing

I have nothing today

No words

No insight

No feelings in anything

In particular

And that's okay

To just be

Breathe in

Breathe out

A day of rest

A day of allowing

Decompress

Binge a show

Read a book

Nap

I have nothing today

And it's wonderful

Here

How long have I been here
In this place
In my head
Mentally
Emotionally
Spinning wheels
Stuck in the mud
Years upon years
Of wallowing
Repeating the same mistakes
Of blaming
Anyone or anything
Other than myself
Of not understanding
What I had to do
How could things change
If I didn't change things
Until one day
I did
Change
What I wanted
How I wanted my life to be
My mindset
I became brave
At least braver than yesterday
I looked in the mirror
In the shadows of my mind
My personality
I began to work
On accepting
The things I didn't like
About me
My thoughts
Integrating
I gave myself a break
Forgave myself for the past
I worked
On change
Of behaviors
Thought process
Perspective
Then
One day
I looked up
I was somewhere new
No longer wallowing in that mud
I keep walking
Sometimes forward

Sometimes backwards

And that's okay

I'm aware of movement

Of becoming who I am

Living in the moment

Step by step

Breath by breath

Unstuck

Change by little change

Pain

Pain is like flowers
It can blossom
It can bloom
It takes sunshine
To make them smile
But it's really the rain
Where the flowers
Grow the most
Just like our pain
And the flowers
They don't last forever
They have their time and place
Flowers need to die for a bit
Only to be reborn
Something new
But still something to behold
Pain is like our soil
We grow out of it
Into something different
Than we were before
Changed
Reincarnated
But still beautiful
Stronger than before
Pain is like
Flowers
A cycle of life

Rain of Tears

It's been raining here
It feels like it's rainy across the world
Maybe it's just storming inside of me
Maybe this rain is just my tears
Finally flowing free
From years of being dammed
Coming forth
Maybe they'll never end
Flooding the Earth
With every emotion
I've ever felt
Maybe I'll drown myself
Or the people in my life
Then again
Maybe I'll finally begin to live
Set free by the rain of love, pain
And everything in between
Let the world flood from the rain within me
Salty like the ocean
And picturesque like a movie scene
Tears slip down my face
Freeing
Loving this open space
To express
To breathe

Mosaic

What is a mosaic
They are beautiful
Meticulously crafted
Stunning once put together
What are they really
But broken pieces
Shattered
A mess
That are crafted together
With patience
And love
Glued into something new
Better
Reformed out of the old
Into a gloriously new thing
Reminiscent of the past
But better
Stronger
Embodying a breathtaking sunrise
New
Bright
All possibilities in front of you
I am the craftsman
Of the mosaic that is me
A work in progress
Redesigning the shape
As I go

Nothing

I have nothing
That I can say
To make it better
There is nothing
I can do
To prove it gets better
Right now
There is no story
No song
No example
Nothing
That will confirm
Things will change
Or improve
BUT
But....
There is hope
That's all I need

That hope
A glimmer
A sliver
A chance
1%
That's it
Then IT can happen
Whatever
can happen
As long as there is hope
Your hope
It, you, anything
Can happen
Keep hope
Alive
Always

Blessing

The shattered clouds

And speckled shadows

Yellow rays from the sun

And the green from the earth

This morning

Breathes life into me

Another day

Another love

Another blessing

Handhold

This is for you
All those that think they are alone
Your eyes are closed
No wonder it seems so dark
Open them up
You'll eventually see
The twinkling lights
Like stars in the sky
The people who are there
To help
Listen
Support when you need it
You feel alone
But you don't need to be
Connection is only an arm's length away
A handhold away
This is for you
You're not alone
Just be willing to see
The world's a big place
Someone is holding a space
For you
And me

Seize

I've been down on my knees

Beaten and bruised

Lost on my path

Nowhere to turn

Caught in a trap

Of my own devising

Voiceless

In a world full of song

Desperate

With nothing to lose

But don't give up hope

You've got so much to do

If you're willing to change

And look in the mirror

Be honest with yourself

Have nothing to prove

Believe in self

March on

Every second

Every breath

Is your chance

Choice

To begin

Renew

So create what you want

Seize the moments

Not the regrets

Healing

Is not for the faint of heart

It requires a bravery

Untested before

I have scratches and bruises

That can't be seen

I fight within my brain

Leaving me scarred and worn

It's not easy

It's not linear

Healing is a winding path

That never ends

Steel yourself

Prepare for a never-ending battle

But the spoils of this war

Is winning your true self back

A treasure unmeasured

Reborn

As the rain washes my soul

Cleansing the old

Freeing me

For what's to come

I secretly smile

Drenched in my own security

Renewed in my own power

That I did not realize was mine

I allow it to baptize this new spirit

My new vision

Let the rain take the burdens

The judgments

Back to the mud

To the Earth

Stand tall now

You are reborn

Reflection

As I gaze at my reflection

In the pool of my life

I relate better to the shadows there

In the depths of those waters

I may not like them

But I love them nonetheless

For they are me

Scared

Alone

Ignorant of what I could be

Of the beauty unrealized

But eventually budding from the seed of my hope

My desire to be better

A better me

A better life

A better world that I can create

Manifest

From the small untended flame of self-love

Flickering

Barely, in that dark place of my inner world

I did not know you were there, love, yearning, straining, crying for release

A love that bursts forth!

Breaking up from the dry cracked ground of fear at the bottom of that pool. Those waters are now feeding it

Slowly but steadily

Those waters

mixed of all

Shadow, fear, hope, pain, happiness, and all things that make up the being of my essence

Together

Accepted

A fragile understanding that creates growth

Inspires the evolution of the self

The soul

That sparked the love and grace of myself

For myself

And those waves I stirred up

In my pool

Washing over and away the debris of my life

The debris that hid this new path I found

This path I now journey

Embarking upon

With new adventure

Discovery

Mountains to climb

Deserts to cross

Roads untraveled

And a life to create as my whole self believes to

Thank you, me!

For being brave!

For taking those first steps into that brave new world

For enduring on, though, it was alien, unknown, and befuddling

For feeling stupid and silly

But not listening to the doubt being whispered in your ear

by that part of you that wanted to protect you

But it did not know what you really needed

Desired

Was change

Transformation

Evolution of self

Thank you me

For being brave enough to face the unknown

And learning to love yourself now

And more in the future

DOMI
STAN

It is my utmost wish that you find hope in it.

Hope in yourself.

Life can be hard sometimes… a lot of times. Don't sugar coat it; shit is shit, but what grows out of it? Beautiful things. Lush greenery. Gorgeous towering trees. Blooming fragrant astounding flowers… and you if you chose to.

Optimism can be your guide. Control what you can, which is you. Your reactions. Your choices.

You're okay, if you choose to be.

I finally did, and it changed the path I walked. That doesn't mean I don't have stumbles or bad days. I do!

But here's to smiles, tears, laughs, and feeling everything we can in life.

Go be better than okay!

Coming soon; a poetic journey with love and all that goes with it.

See you there!

About the Author

Scott Thornton is a devoted husband to his wife, Laura, and a proud father to their two delightful children, John and Tegan. He shares his home with two loyal companions: Mister Harry, an energetic Australian Shepherd, and Lola, a spunky Chihuahua. Scott is an entrepreneur, and co-owner of a successful plumbing wholesale company, where his leadership and passion for business shine.

Throughout his life, Scott has been a passionate lover of comic books and superheroes, with a particular fondness for *Star Wars* and Funko Pops, especially those of Thor. His love for imagination, fantasy, and science fiction fuels his creative spirit and keeps him connected to his inner child.

Despite his vibrant interests, Scott's life has not always been easy. He struggled to cope with grief after the passing of his grandmother, a loss that took him over twenty years to fully process. During this time, Scott turned to alcohol as a way to numb the pain and avoid confronting difficult emotions. But in a life-changing moment, he made the courageous decision to stop drinking cold turkey.

It was at this pivotal juncture that Scott found guidance from Pauline Nguyen, the Spiritual Entrepreneur, whose wisdom opened new pathways to healing. Through her mentorship, Scott began to tackle his suppressed emotions, challenge his inner critic, and cultivate self-love. Writing poetry became an essential outlet for him to express his feelings and process his journey. This is where his path as a writer truly began.

Through his struggles, Scott learned that he was not alone in his feelings of unhappiness and being lost in life. With determination, self-compassion, and the help of others, he began to transform his life, discovering that he had the power to create change. Today, over four years sober, Scott's core values are authenticity, humor, personal growth, and creativity. He is deeply passionate about helping others, finding immense fulfillment in supporting those on their own journeys toward healing and self-discovery.

Above all, Scott's greatest joy is his family, and it is through them-and his dedication to living a life of purpose-that he continues to grow, heal, and inspire others.

Acknowledgements

There are some people I need to thank...

Pauline Nguyen, the Spiritual Entrepreneur.

A shaman. A raven. A blessing.

Thank you for feeling my pain and accepting the call to help guide me through. For showing me there are different paths, and that we can see with more than our eyes. You are wise, funny, curse a lot (which I greatly appreciate), brutally honest with a purpose, and wonderfully kind. Thank you for your lessons even when they don't land immediately. They land when they land. Thank you. I love you.

Yvette Tarrant.

I can't begin to express the depth of my gratitude. You helped me walk through a grief so deep, I hadn't even realized I had drowned in it. I tear up as I write this because it stirs so much emotion. "Thank you" does not do justice to what you gave me, but thank you anyway. Through your steady, patient, persistent guidance, I finally saw a light at the end of a tunnel I thought had no ending. Your mischievous laugh and the twinkle in your eyes made our sessions bearable, even when you made me want to scream. I will always think of you kindly, and consider you an angel in human form. Thank you. I love you.

Hallie Avolio, SassyHealthyFit.

You came into my life when I desperately needed a bright light, a cheerleader, someone who could convince me I was capable, worthy, and enough. You helped me discover and define core values I didn't even know were hidden inside me. You believed in me when I couldn't believe in myself. You also swear a lot, which I love, and you are absolutely a 100% no-bullshitter. Your enthusiasm and optimism helped ignite mine again. I hope we never lose touch. Thank you. I love you.

Robert Presbrey. Always SFM.

You are my brother, though we aren't related by blood. It's a bond deeper than that. Thank you for always being there for me, especially when I didn't deserve it. We are peas in a pod, almost the same person. You crack me up and have one of the kindest hearts I've ever known. Let more people see that. You deserve all the happiness you seek—just be sure that happiness is worthy of someone as incredible as you. Uncle Rob to my kids, and dishwasher for my wife—you'll always be family. Thank you. I love you.

Grandma.

You were the best of everything. The brightest, shiniest light in my world. You showed me the meaning of unconditional love. Without you, I don't know where I would have ended up. You are everything good in me. I miss you still. It took me time to understand that you are always with me, and that I don't have to live in sadness. Your lessons and your love have always been inside me. I only wish my children could have met you and known your wonder, but it's up to me to show it to them. Thank you. I love you.

These writings, poems, and expressions are my heart and soul's journey, walking in and out of the light.
This journey is never-ending.
I will always be made of both light and dark.
And that's okay. That's life. All parts of life.

These words have saved my sanity and my life.
They hold deep meaning and silly irreverence.
They speak of grief, loss, anger, love, disappointment, heartbreak, desire, pain, addiction, and everything else we feel as humans.

I hope they are enjoyed.
But in truth, it doesn't really matter.

They aren't mine anymore.
They belong to the world, to the universe, to the wind and to you, should you choose to receive them.

Thank you.

Art Index

Sharon Daugherty

Sharon Daugherty is a Philadelphia-born painter and sketch artist. The self-taught artist uses abstract expressionism to honor feminine energy and human experience, and to examine how we interact with our environments. Her subjects range from abstract portraits and human figures to urban landscapes. She is a color specialist who loves highly expressive and textural work, using acrylic, gouache, watercolor, ink, charcoal, and other materials on a variety of surfaces. Her work is highly intuitive, reacting to what the canvas gives her as she works.

Sharon's work is collected by people around the world. As she finds painting a highly therapeutic medium for herself, she also works with students to help them discover the power of creative expression. Sharon is part of a family of creatives – a husband who is a writer and musician, and two daughters, one a sculptor and writer, and one a singer-songwriter. She works out of her home studio where her family gives her constant energy, inspiration, and support. Find her work at www.sharondartist.com

Artwork for: Cover, Lonely (Pg. 19), Ribbons (Pg. 167), Damaged Goods (Pg. 185), Water Colors (Pg. 208)

Bella Rootz

Bella Rootz is a 35-year-old self-taught artist and painter based in Gainesville, Florida. With a natural passion for creativity and expression, Bella has carved her own path in the art world, selling over 200 paintings to collectors and art lovers across the country. Her work, vibrant and deeply personal, reflects a lifetime of dedication to her craft and a profound respect for the power of art to heal, inspire, and transform.

As a devoted mother to two beautiful children—a daughter and a son—Bella finds endless inspiration in their fresh perspectives and boundless curiosity. They are her daily reminder to see the world through new eyes, fueling her imagination and deepening her connection to her work.

Art has had a profoundly positive impact on Bella's life, serving as both a sanctuary and a form of self-discovery. Now, she is fully committed to building her passion into a lifelong career, sharing her vision with the world and, encouraging others to find beauty in the everyday. Through her journey, Bella Rootz continues to prove that with heart, resilience, and authenticity, creativity can truly change lives.

https://www.instagram.com/bella.rootz/

Artwork for: Ooze (Pg. 9), Cracks (Pg. 79), Pieces (Pg. 87), Broken Mirrors (Pg. 145), Eyes Open (Pg. 155)

Dominika Stanczak

When I create, I always start from a heartfelt space.
I do not confine myself to technical constrictions, perfection, or correctness.
I do not concentrate on the outcome but rather allow myself to flow with the lines, shapes, and layers of very intense colours in visual experiments and the stream of words in their linguistic counterparts, which reflect the turbulences and passion for life I love experiencing on a deep, soulful level.

I immerse myself in the story of the painting or writing as if I were embodying a story from my own life, which I now want to experience more reflectively.

https://domistan.com/

https://www.instagram.com/domi_stan/

Artwork for: Oxidized (Pg. 85), Awake (Pg. 179), Envy (Pg. 193), Reflection (Pg. 227)

Hope Tian

Born and raised in Beijing, China, artist Hope Tian is a self-taught oil painter for over 12 years. While pursuing a graduate degree in New York State, she answered a lifelong calling of becoming a professional visual Artist. Now residing in the Boston area, she spends her days expanding her already vast repertoire of oil paintings, collaborating with gallery owners and educational institutions, supporting not-for-profit organizations, and partnering with international classical performing Artists. Most recently, Hope Tian is a featured Artist at The Gallery at Jimmy's https://jimmysoncongress.com/the-gallery-at-jimmys/ and was also the guest Artist on Jane King's broadcast on The Fox Business Network, Bloomberg TV, and Newsmax.

Artist Hope Tian finds great excitement and creativity in the exploration of varied subjects and eclectic styles of oil painting. The range of her Artwork goes from impressionistic or post-impressionistic to expressionistic or Fauvist, to truly representational to abstract. Hope's paintings are heavily influenced by her keen interest in and ongoing study of the master painters.

https://www.hopetianart.com/

https://www.instagram.com/hope.tian/

https://www.linkedin.com/in/hope-t-76a363185/?utm_source=share&utm_campaign=share_via&utm_content=profile&utm_medium=ios_app

https://www.facebook.com/hope.tian.50?mibextid=kFxxJD

Artwork for: Adrift (Pg. 101), Alone in Bed (Pg. 151), Give Up (Pg. 207)

Elaine Lore

Elaine Lóre is a Czech painter who mainly deals with expressive painting and painting her worlds. Her work is characterized mainly by a wide palette of colors or, conversely, a complete minimum, when she is experiencing a darker period in her life. From this period is the painting Emptiness, which reflects the depressive period of the past days. You can find her work on the website

https://www.elainelore.cz/en/

Artwork for: Wiped Away (Pg. 17)

Lena Podmark Art

Contemporary artist.

Can be found on Instagram @lena_podmark_art

Artwork for: Over and Over (Pg. 51), Attention (Pg. 189), Rain of Tears (Pg. 215), Handhold (Pg. 221), Messy (Pg. 13)

Ning Liando

Ning Liando is an illustrator and painter who explores themes of vulnerability and emotion through her work, creating pieces that resonate with the human experience. Her art is also a reflection of her own.

https://www.instagram.com/sass_at_studio/

Artwork for: Blame (Pg. 47), Sadness (Pg. 55), Poetry (Pg. 91), No Words (Pg. 111), Black Tar (Pg. 173)

Somniodelic Workshop

Astral dreamscapes through the prismatic lensing of consciousness.
Cybermages.
Somnio (Latin): dream
Delic (Greek): to manifest

https://www.facebook.com/profile.php?id=100086307742543

Artwork for: Demons (Pg. 67)

Austin Wafer

I'm just a storyteller.

From Texas

https://www.austinwafer.com/

https://www.instagram.com/austinwafer/

Artwork for: Crown of Pain (Pg. 69)

Gregg Babus

Thank you for your art contributions.

Everything is art.
Especially ourselves.

https://www.instagram.com/gregg_babus/

Artwork for: Pain (Pg. 213), Feel (Pg. 187)

Sheeba Khan

Her eclectic mix of vivid abstracts captures the vibrance of her colorful childhood. Each of her deeply layered pieces embodies a myriad of stories, letting the beholder find a new interpretation with every fresh look. With audacious colors and passionate storytelling, she has garnered rave reviews from the art community across the world. A collection of her work is currently being exhibited in Montclair (New Jersey). NYC, London, Milan, and Dubai at prestigious galleries.

https://www.artbysheebakhan.com/

Artwork for: Devoid (Pg. 25)

Eric Ravenwolf

My name is Eric. I'm an artist, Swiftie, and mental health advocate from San Antonio, Texas. I've been doing art for a few years, and I hope you find it as healing for you as it has been for me.

https://www.theartsybrain.com/

https://www.instagram.com/the_artsy_brain/

Artwork for: Ego (Pg. 23), Buried Alive (Pg. 41), Haunted (Pg. 97), Setting Fire (Pg. 107), Empty Space (Pg. 137), Fire (Pg. 177)

Bookwithnoname

Thai artist, fashionista, and punk.
https://www.instagram.com/bookwithnoname/

Email: sridaaa@hotmail.com

Artwork for: Door (Pg. 117)

Scott Thornton

Author of this book.

Artwork for: Dark Creatures (Pg. 75), Golden Road (Pg. 146)

Resources for Healing

Pauline Nguyen

Developmental Coach

"Personal Development cannot happen unless Personal Disruption happens first."

Pauline Nguyen is a conscious entrepreneur, international keynote speaker, and life coach who integrates science and spirituality into her life, her teachings, and her coaching.

Her exclusive techniques support people in search of balance, peace, and purpose in their lives. A Shamanic practitioner, she uses her profound knowledge of ancient wisdom to call on healing and transformative energies, to assist her clients and students in gaining clarity, accessing their power, and making profound and lasting changes in their lives.

https://pauline-nguyen.com/

https://pauline-nguyen.com/numinous/

Yvette Tarrant

Yvette Tarrant Coaching

Transition Coach
Life is in the transitions
Reset | Reclaim | Rise 🧡
Death| Divorce| Empty Nesting| Midlife Crisis |Career Change🔶Certified Coach

https://www.instagram.com/yvettetarrantcoaching/

https://www.facebook.com/p/Yvette-Tarrant-Coaching-100084528371247/

Alene McDowell-Ibanez

Counseling Services

McDowell-Ibanez Counseling Services is a private psychotherapy practice dedicated to providing compassionate and professional mental health services to individuals seeking support and guidance through challenging life situations. At McDowell-Ibanez Counseling Services, my mission is to empower individuals to lead fulfilling lives by promoting mental and emotional well-being through evidence-based psychotherapy.

https://therapys.org/

www.ingramcontent.com/pod-product-compliance
Lightning Source LLC
LaVergne TN
LVHW070909210926
848482LV00017B/1029